Remarkable Woodpeckers

INCREDIBLE IMAGES AND CHARACTERISTICS

BY STAN TEKIELA

Adventure Publications, Inc.
Cambridge, MN

DEDICATION

Behind every author is an editor who makes the writing clear and concise without taking any personal credit. Without the editor, the author is just another writer. This book is dedicated to my editor, Sandy Livoti, who has spent over a decade helping my words say what I mean. Thanks, my friend, for being there for me.

ACKNOWLEDGMENTS

The following people and organizations have been instrumental in obtaining many of the amazing images in this book. Thank you, one and all, for all that you do.

Don Anderson • Deborah Dailey Billmeier • Bird Collection, Bell Museum of Natural History, University of Minnesota (St. Paul) • Rick and Nora Bowers • Jeff Cordes • Sue Fletcher • Phil Jenni, Jessika Madison-Kennedy and Tami Vogel of the Wildlife Rehabilitation Center of Minnesota (Roseville) • Karla Kinstler • Mike Lentz • David C. Olson

Special thanks to Rick Bowers, author, bird expert, wildlife photographer and friend, for reviewing this book. Your extensive knowledge of woodpeckers is greatly appreciated.

Cover photos by Stan Tekiela

All photos by Stan Tekiela except pp. 30 and 72 by Jim Zipp, pg. 80 by Sue Fletcher, pp. 81, 98 and 143 (Lewis's, Red-breasted, White-headed) by Brian E. Small and pg. 134 by Irvin LeBlanc. Some photos were taken under controlled conditions.

Edited by Sandy Livoti

Cover and book design by Jonathan Norberg

10 9 8 7 6 5 4 3 2 1

Copyright 2011 by Stan Tekiela
Published by Adventure Publications, Inc.
820 Cleveland St. S
Cambridge, MN 55008
1-800-678-7006
www.adventurepublications.net
All rights reserved
Printed in China

ISBN: 978-1-59193-321-2

TABLE OF CONTENTS

Remarkable Woodpeckers.........................5

The Woodpecker Family.........................6

Family Traits.........................7

A Good Name.........................10

Origins of the Species.........................12

Sizes Small to Great.........................14

Life Span.........................17

Staying Alive.........................20

Woodpeckers from Coast to Coast.........22

Essential Habitat.........................23

Differences of the Sexes.........................25

Stylish Plumage.........................30

Flap-Bounding Flight.........................34

Flight Sounds.........................35

Head Hammering.........................36

Unique Skull.........................40

Bill Shock.........................42

Self-Sharpening Beak.........................46

Nostril Filters.........................47

Eye Safety.........................47

Sighting Skills.........................48

Tongue Bones.........................50

Customized Tongues.........................51

Muscles to Ribs.........................56

Fancy Feet.........................57

Leg Positioning.........................58

Tail Bracing.........................59

Hitching Up Trees.........................62

What's for Dinner?.........................65

Hawking.........................67

The Food Pantry.........................68

Sap Taps.........................75

Preening.........................77

Quick Baths.........................79

Sunning.........................80

Call Notes.........................81

Drumming to Communicate.................84

Sapsucker Migration.........................88

Woodpecker Territories.........................89

Nest—New or Old?.........................92

Specialized Cavities.........................94

Choosing a Nest Site.........................98

Cavity Excavation.........................100

Wood Chip Disposal.........................101

Chamber Entrance.........................104

Roosting Habits.........................105

Visual Displays.........................108

Mating Encounters.........................112

White Eggshells.........................113

Small Eggs.........................114

Eggs on Schedule.........................114

Egg Layers.........................115

Clutch Diversity.........................116

Incubation Day and Night...................118

Brood Patch.........................120

Temperature Control.........................121

Time to Hatch.........................122

Cooperative Brooding.........................124

Feeding the Young.........................126

Fecal Sacs.........................132

Fledgling Appearance.........................133

Independence.........................135

Attracting Woodpeckers.........................138

The Wonder of Woodpeckers...............140

Featured Woodpeckers.........................142

About the Author.........................144

Downy Woodpecker

There are many unusual birds in the world, but there is one group of highly specialized birds that I find incredibly interesting—the woodpeckers. Woodpeckers are found in a wide variety of habitats, from jungles to thick forests to parched deserts, and even into some grasslands. They are the carpenters of the bird world, creating nest cavities in trees each year—an important task since many cavity-nesting birds can't excavate their own and depend on the handiwork of woodpeckers for their survival. In addition, woodpeckers eat countless tons of insects, greatly minimizing pest damage to forests.

Woodpeckers have unique shapes, making them easily recognizable by any and all who see them. Their special features and behaviors have captured my attention as a naturalist and wildlife photographer for over 20 years. Here is their remarkable story.

Woodpeckers are found all around the world except in New Guinea, Antarctica, Australia, New Zealand, Madagascar and on smaller islands. The woodpecker family, called Picidae, is composed of a large group of birds with similar unique traits. Within this family are three subfamilies. The Jynginae subfamily, or wrynecks, occurs exclusively in Europe, Asia and Africa. The Picumninae, or piculets, is a subfamily of tropical woodpeckers seen in Southeast Asia, Africa and the South American tropics. The Picinae subfamily, known as true woodpeckers (picids), is the most common and widespread, and includes flickers and sapsuckers. Since there are no wrynecks or piculets in United States and Canada, this book will consider only the picids—the true woodpeckers.

Red-headed Woodpecker

There are nearly 200 species of true woodpeckers, each sharing strikingly similar characteristics. They are all considered primary cavity nesters, which means they have the ability to excavate their own cavities in trees for nesting.

All woodpeckers share traits that aid in excavation. The head is designed to withstand repeated hammering against a tree without causing brain damage. The bill is long and chisel-like—perfect for removing small pieces of wood or probing into cracks and crevices. The tongue is very long with a modified tip for snaking into small holes and extracting insects. Nostrils are covered with specialized feathers to keep out dust and dirt. Short legs and strong toes are ideal for clinging tightly to vertical surfaces during hammering with the beak. The tail is long and stiff and acts like the third leg of a tripod, which is key to the bird's stability when hammering holes in trees. A couple ribs are abnormally large, enabling extra muscle attachment, easing the tough job of excavation. All of these features are unique to woodpeckers and make them extraordinary birds indeed.

Woodpeckers are masters at locating insects tucked in crevices and cracks and under the bark of upright trees. Of the nearly 10,000 bird species worldwide, only a handful of species besides woodpeckers obtain food this way. The White-breasted Nuthatch is one of the few birds that has mastered the art of hunting insects on a vertical tree trunk like a woodpecker. Given the competition for sparse food, it's no wonder that woodpeckers are so successful and widespread in the bird world.

Hairy Woodpecker

A GOOD NAME

The common name for most birds is often a fairly accurate description of a physical characteristic or activity. For example, woodcreepers creep along wood, and hummingbirds create a humming noise during flight. Woodpeckers are known for pecking wood while probing a tree for insects, but you could make an argument against the name because woodpeckers don't just peck wood—they actually whack, hack or chisel it. In fact, it's really more accurate to say they hammer wood. Sometimes the hammering is so intense, they smash the wood.

However you describe it, woodpeckers are amazing. They create large, gaping holes in one of nature's most solid and durable materials, and they do it with just the beaks on their faces—a truly astonishing feat!

Red-bellied Woodpecker

Northern Flicker

ORIGINS OF THE SPECIES

Like many other bird species, the exact origins of this group of birds are not known. We do know, however, that members of the Picidae family, called picids, are some of the most ancient of all birds. As evidence, a woodpecker feather encased in amber dates back 24 million years, and a fossilized woodpecker leg bone from Germany is estimated to be 25 million years old. Nest cavities excavated in petrified trees in Arizona, which are thought to be 50 million years old, indicate that these birds have been around for a very long time.

The DNA analysis of nearly 3,000 woodpeckers indicates that the origins of some may have started in the Old World. However, the geographical origin of the true woodpeckers (picids) might have begun in the New World.

Woodpeckers have no close relatives. Evidence suggests that woodpeckers branched off from other birds about 50–53 million years ago. Since then, they have evolved to be highly specialized birds that are extremely successful. While all ancient woodpecker species are extinct, all woodpecker species we see today have been around for many millions of years.

Pileated Woodpecker

SIZES SMALL TO GREAT

Woodpecker size ranges from the tiny Downy Woodpecker, which is just over 6 inches long, to the crow-sized Pileated Woodpecker, at about 17 inches. Many of our woodpeckers average 7–8 inches in length. Several of these medium-sized birds are the Arizona, Nuttall's and Ladder-backed Woodpeckers. Red-bellied, White-headed and Black-backed Woodpeckers are slightly larger at 9–10 inches, along with the Downy's look-alike larger cousin, the Hairy Woodpecker. Flickers are the next largest, with Gilded Flickers measuring about 11 inches, and Northern Flickers, 12–13 inches. All sapsuckers, such as Yellow-bellied and Red-breasted Sapsuckers, share a similar size, around 8–9 inches.

Downy Woodpecker

Acorn Woodpecker

Generally, the larger the bird, the longer it lives. A minuscule hummingbird, for instance, is the smallest of all birds and has a short, fast life of 2–5 years. The California Condor, our largest bird, lives around 75–80 years. Woodpeckers have a short to medium life span. Most live about 5–10 years, with some reaching 20 years. The small Downy Woodpecker, for example, lives only 5–8 years. Larger Red-bellied Woodpeckers live about 12 years, Hairy Woodpeckers can survive longer, up to 15½ years, and Acorn Woodpeckers, which are even larger, 16 years. The life span of our largest woodpecker, the Pileated, ranges between 10–20 years.

Red-bellied Woodpecker

Hairy Woodpecker

The reproductive success of woodpeckers is slightly higher than that of other bird species. Most have about a 60 percent survival rate for each batch, or brood, of young. Other species of birds average around 50 percent. This means that if six Red-bellied Woodpecker eggs hatch successfully, only 3–4 young will make it through their first year of life. Once a woodpecker has reached its first hatch-day (1 year of age), the chances of it surviving to live a full, productive life are very good.

Woodpeckers have a slight advantage over other birds in the early stages of life. Because they are cavity dwellers, their vulnerability to predators and wet, cold weather is significantly reduced. Cavity dwelling provides an excellent refuge for incubating, hatching and fledging young birds. After fledging, the playing field becomes more level with other bird species, with young woodpeckers suffering similar mortality rates.

Staying alive is not easy for a young woodpecker. Learning to fly and find food is very hard, and the consequences of not mastering these skills is always death. When young woodpeckers leave the nest cavity, they often can't fly more than a short distance and must rely on their feet to cling to tree trunks. One false step and the birds can end up on the ground, where many ground-dwelling predators will snap them up.

Fast-flying Cooper's Hawks and other woodland hawks that eat other birds seem to prefer woodpeckers for their meals. Cooper's Hawks target flickers and other wood-peckers disproportionately over other birds, possibly because woodpeckers are fairly large and not fast flyers, making them easy pickings.

Golden-fronted Woodpecker

WOODPECKERS FROM COAST TO COAST

Of the nearly 200 true woodpeckers species, 22 are found in the United States and Canada. This excludes the elusive Ivory-billed Woodpecker, which hasn't been proven conclusively to still exist.

Some woodpeckers, such as Downy and Hairy Woodpeckers, occur in just about any habitat across the country. Nuttall's Woodpecker, on the other hand, is found only in California and Mexico. Other species, such as the Lewis's Woodpecker, require higher elevations, while still others live only in the desert. Gila Woodpeckers, for instance, are southwestern desert dwellers, and Arizona Woodpeckers are seen only in a small and highly restricted area of the American Southwest.

Gila Woodpecker

ESSENTIAL HABITAT

Woodpeckers need one thing for their habitat—trees. In general, if an environment lacks trees, woodpeckers will be absent. Large woodpeckers, such as the Pileated, require big trees. In smaller woodpecker species, large or small trees will do. A variety of tree sizes is necessary for an assortment of woodpeckers to call a particular area home. One desert dweller, however—the Gila Woodpecker—resides in saguaro cacti and doesn't rely on trees at all.

Red-headed Woodpecker

DIFFERENCES OF THE SEXES

There are only three woodpecker species in the United States in which the male and female look alike—the Red-headed Woodpecker, Lewis's Woodpecker and Red-breasted Sapsucker. These species are called sexually monochromatic.

The males and females of all other U.S. woodpecker species are sexually dichromatic, meaning they are different in coloration only, not size. In many species, male woodpeckers have an extra mark, such as a colorful badge, that distinguishes them from the females of their species. For example, male Hairy Woodpeckers have a red spot on the back of the head that the Hairy females lack. Golden-fronted Woodpecker males have a red mark on top of the head, while the entire crown of Red-bellied Woodpecker males is red. Male Red-cockaded Woodpeckers have a tiny red badge (cockade) on the head that is hidden from view except during excitement. Pileated Woodpecker males have two marks of distinction—red mustache marks near the back of the beak and a red forehead.

male Pileated Woodpecker

female Pileated Woodpecker

male Williamson's Sapsucker

female Williamson's Sapsucker

In flickers, which are mostly brown, males have red or black marks behind the beak. Differences in sapsuckers show mainly on the male throat, which is red, not white, like the female sapsucker throat. Williamson's Sapsucker is the most sexually dichromatic woodpecker, with females looking so markedly different from the black and white males that they don't even appear to be the same species.

Lewis's Woodpecker

STYLISH PLUMAGE

Nearly all woodpeckers are a bold combination of black and white, with a splash of red or yellow on the males. The glossy green Lewis's Woodpecker, with its red face and gray collar, is the only exception in the United States to the usual striking black and white plumage. Of course, this doesn't take into account the flickers, which are muted shades of brown.

The black color in the plumage comes from a pigment that gives feathers additional strength and durability. Strong feathers are absolutely necessary for birds that spend so much time in contact with rough tree bark. Sturdy feathers are also needed to withstand nest cavity activity, which involves full body contact and constant friction with the tree.

Northern Flicker

Downy Woodpecker

Pileated Woodpecker

Pileated Woodpecker

FLAP-BOUNDING FLIGHT

Woodpeckers have a unique flight pattern that makes them easy to identify from a distance. Their flight is unlike most other birds, which flap continuously, producing a straight or level flight. Woodpeckers fly in a distinctive undulating pattern, called flap-bounding, consisting of a flap phase followed by a bounding phase. The flap phase lasts just a few seconds and causes the woodpecker to rise. In the bounding phase, the bird tucks in its wings and takes a short, free ride. Altitude is lost during the glide, making the flight pattern over a long distance appear roller coaster-like—ascending when flapping and descending when free-riding.

FLIGHT SOUNDS

Woodpeckers also have unique feathers. The feathers in the wings and especially the tail are much stiffer than those of other birds. They are so rigid that they create a unique sound during flight in concert with friction and moving air. They actually rub against each other loudly enough to produce a clamoring noise similar to the sound of thin wooden sticks clacking together. This is such a distinctive sound, it is possible to know when a woodpecker is in the area just by hearing it fly.

There are many specialized features of our wonderful woodpeckers. The head is one of the most important because it is used for the essential tasks of finding food and creating nest cavities.

How woodpeckers chisel holes in trees without incurring brain damage has intrigued people for hundreds of years. When a woodpecker delivers a blow to a tree trunk, the bill strikes at a speed sufficient to cause all sorts of damage to the bill, the skull and especially the brain. A typical strike speed by an average woodpecker is about 20–24 feet per second. A car crash is survivable at a maximum G-force of about 100 G's of deceleration at impact. In larger woodpeckers, such as the Pileated, the force of the deceleration at impact has been measured at an astonishing 600–1,500 G's! Given that the average woodpecker strikes its beak about 100–200 times a minute over many hours and many days, it's a miracle that these birds are not constantly suffering brain damage upon impact.

Hairy Woodpecker

Yellow-bellied Sapsucker

A 1976 study published in *The Lancet* medical journal found that the brain of a typical woodpecker is relatively small and lightweight compared with its body. The force of impact to such a small brain is distributed over a greater surface, reducing the chance of brain injury by as much as 100 times. Thus, no matter how fast the head is moving, the woodpecker brain simply lacks the mass to develop enough inertia to cause major damage.

The skull of a woodpecker is different from any other bird. Woodpeckers have a bone projecting above the base of the upper bill, resulting in a rounded forehead rather than a sloping forehead, which is seen in other birds. This bone acts like a stop, or block, for the upper bill. Like other bird bills, the upper bill, or upper mandible, of a woodpecker is movable or hinged. The action of the hinge, which allows the upper mandible to move independently of the skull, is called cranial kinesis. Cranial kinesis could be a major liability for a woodpecker each time it crashes its bill into a tree, but the frontal bone helps to keep the upper mandible in place.

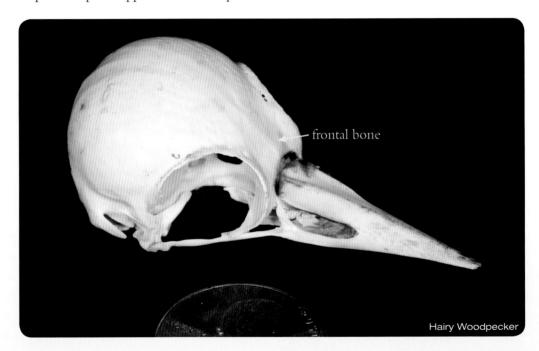

frontal bone

Hairy Woodpecker

Black-backed Woodpecker

Northern Flicker

The woodpecker species that do the most excavating, such as Black-backed Woodpeckers, have the largest frontal bones. Flickers have the smallest frontal bones since most of their feeding occurs on the ground, gathering ants.

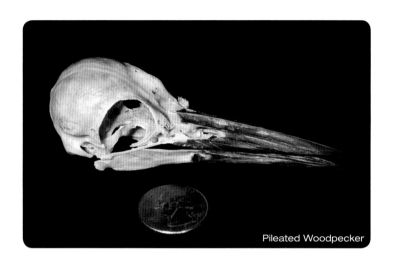
Pileated Woodpecker

BILL SHOCK

Woodpeckers also have additional cartilage between the bill and the skull that helps to absorb shock during hammering activity. In addition, they have a large muscle, called the protractor muscle, that is attached to the base of the upper bill. Woodpeckers that do more strenuous excavating have a larger protractor muscle. This muscle contracts just before each impact and absorbs much of the shock in addition to holding the bill steady.

Woodpeckers that excavate extensively for insects, such as Pileated Woodpeckers, have a long, pointed bill. The bill size and shape dictates how it is used for excavation. Each blow to the tree is delivered perpendicularly to the wood. In fact, if you were to draw a line through the length of the bill, it would meet the wood at a perfect right angle. Straight blows prevent the head from rotating to one side or the other during each impact and keep the bill from glancing off to the side, causing shearing injuries. Straight blows also concentrate the force, making each strike more energy effective.

Damage to the brain is not only reduced by the shape of the skull, but also by the attachment of the bill to a specific area. Bill placement on the head is such that each time the bill strikes a tree, the shock wave created by the impact is transmitted in a line through the skull just below the brain, which helps to protect it from excessive vibration.

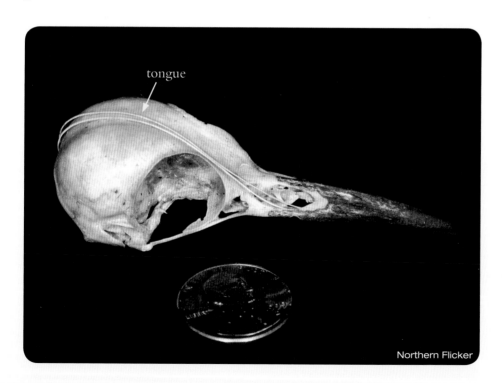

tongue

Northern Flicker

Red-bellied Woodpecker

Hairy Woodpecker

SELF-SHARPENING BEAK

The basic structure of a woodpecker bill is similar to other bird beaks. The hard, bony inner structure is covered with a durable sheath called the ramphotheca. This is a rapidly growing, leathery sheath that grows out like fingernails, from the base, and which is thicker at the base and tapers toward the tip. The tip is continually worn away by the day-to-day activity of feeding, with the abrasion against rugged wood keeping the beak constantly sharp. Woodpeckers take full advantage of this self-sharpening—especially Black-backed Woodpeckers, which are constantly chiseling off bark flakes in search of beetle larvae hidden beneath.

Black-backed Woodpecker

NOSTRIL FILTERS

All birds have nostrils, usually at the base of the bill. Woodpeckers contend with special respiratory challenges, however, because while excavating holes, they must breathe at the same time. Fortunately, they have the benefit of specialized feathers covering their nostrils, which look and act like hairs. These tiny hair-like feathers act like a filter, allowing air to pass through, but not debris. This asset provides excellent protection against the flying dust and wood chips produced during excavation.

Downy Woodpecker

Downy Woodpecker

EYE SAFETY

There is also a safety challenge to the eyes when a woodpecker is drilling for food or excavating cavities. Woodpeckers close their eyes tightly for an instant just before each blow is delivered to a tree. While this happens repeatedly and literally in a blink of an eye, rapid blinking is absolutely necessary to keep the eyes safe and dust-free.

SIGHTING SKILLS

The eyes are located on the sides of a woodpecker's head, allowing the most visibility to the left and right. Since woodpeckers often have a large tree directly in front of them, blocking the forward vision, sideways visibility is a great asset. It helps them see predators that might be approaching from behind or along the sides. Only a small percentage of their vision comes from binocular vision, which is directly in front.

In general, all woodpeckers have excellent color vision. This is apparent by the fact that many woodpeckers are colorful and the males have some kind of bright feathered spot to indicate their sex. A woodpecker's eyesight is like that of other birds of similar size and is considered to be very good. They depend on it to navigate through forests, see predators, locate food and find a mate.

Northern Flicker

49

TONGUE BONES

Tongues of birds are very different from those of mammals. A bird's tongue is composed of a group of long, slender, flexible bones with a soft, fleshy tip, collectively called the hyoid apparatus. The hyoid apparatus in woodpeckers is highly developed due to extra muscle attachments for the extra long flexible bones, which allow them to extend and retract their tongues much farther than other birds. At the base of the tongue, the hyoid apparatus splits into two branches called horns. Here the hyoid is wrapped in muscle and connective tissue, while the horns curl under the jaw and wrap around the base of the skull, extending over the top of the skull and meeting near the nostrils at the base of the bill.

hyoid apparatus

Red-headed Woodpecker

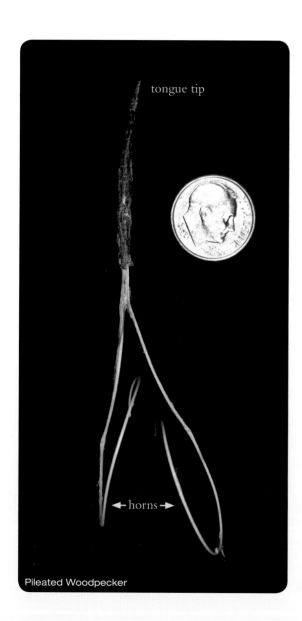

tongue tip

horns

Pileated Woodpecker

CUSTOMIZED TONGUES

Woodpeckers use their tongues to probe deep inside trees to locate and extract insects. Flickers have the longest tongues of all the woodpeckers in the United States and Canada. They can extend their tongues to nearly 2 inches beyond the tip of the bill. Sapsuckers have relatively short tongues that reach only 1 inch past the bill tip. Pileated Woodpeckers have very long tongues that measure almost 2 inches beyond their bill tips, which they use to extract insects hiding deep in cracks and crevices.

The woodpecker tongue tip varies slightly among species, but in all cases it maximizes food gathering. The tip is packed with nerve endings, making it highly sensitive. Many woodpeckers don't see their food, but can feel insects hiding in a tree with the tips of their tongues. Many woodpeckers also have backward-pointing, stiff barbs that securely impale hidden insects and help to draw them out of tight confines. The Golden-fronted Woodpecker, for example, spears and extracts insects with its densely barbed tongue.

Golden-fronted Woodpecker

Woodpeckers that feed mainly on ants, such as the Northern Flicker, have well-developed salivary glands that secrete a sticky saliva, which coats the tongue. The sticky tongue helps the birds catch several ants at a time. Not only that, their saliva is alkaline and counters the acidic defense of the ants.

Other woodpeckers, such as Acorn Woodpeckers and all sapsucker species, have a collection of small hair-like projections at the tip of the tongue, similar to a paintbrush. These projections help them lap up and hold large amounts of tree sap, a favorite food, in the same way a paintbrush holds paint. In addition, the sapsucker tongue has a groove along the sides to funnel or channel sap to the back of the mouth, where it is swallowed.

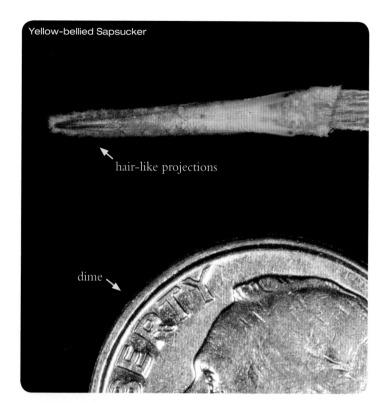

Yellow-bellied Sapsucker

hair-like projections

dime

Red-bellied Woodpecker

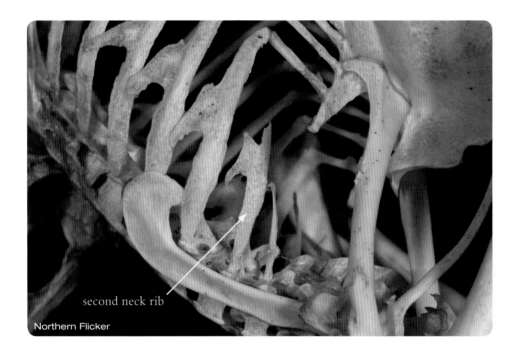

second neck rib

Northern Flicker

MUSCLES TO RIBS

Rib cages in most birds consist of six pairs of ribs (thoracic), which attach in
the front to the breastbone (sternum) and in the back to the spinal column, plus
two pairs of neck ribs (cervical), which attach only in the back to the neck. In
woodpeckers, the second neck rib is notably wider and heavier than it is in other
birds. Woodpeckers that spend most of their time chiseling off bark in search
of food, such as the Black-backed Woodpecker, need extra neck muscles. These
muscles attach at the heavier, second neck rib. Woodpeckers that dig insects out of
the ground, such as flickers, lack strong neck muscles and have slightly less well-
developed neck ribs.

Pileated Woodpecker

Northern Flicker

The feet of woodpeckers are another key to their success in the vertical world. It's not easy to climb up a tree trunk, no matter how simple a woodpecker makes it appear. Holding onto a tree while pulling beetle larvae out from under the bark is another trick that many other birds cannot perform.

Normal toe arrangement in most bird species is three toes pointing forward and one larger toe, called the hallux, pointing back. This works well for birds that spend most of their time on horizontal surfaces, such as the ground and outstretched tree branches, but woodpeckers spend their lives vertically, sticking to trees like Velcro after landing on trunks and branches upright.

Except for the American Three-toed and Black-backed Woodpeckers, woodpeckers have two toes pointing forward and two pointing back. This toe arrangement, called zygodactyl, provides extra downward-facing toe power, which aids in the ability to cling to a vertical object. One of the two toes pointing backward (the fourth toe) is flexible and also splays to the side. This fourth toe provides even more stability and gripping power in many different clinging situations, including keeping the bird firmly attached while it is hammering hard at a tree with its beak.

Pileated Woodpecker

LEG POSITIONING

In addition to the special arrangement of the feet, woodpeckers also have a unique way of positioning their legs while hanging onto a tree. Large woodpeckers, such as Pileated Woodpeckers, hold their legs slightly splayed to the sides when perching, as if to hug the tree. When the woodpecker's heels are in direct contact with the trunk, the body is drawn in closer, increasing tail feather contact with the tree and greatly reducing the effect of gravity on the woodpecker. Thus, the legs work in concert with the tail to provide even more upright perching stability.

TAIL BRACING

Clinging to the sides of trees seems natural and effortless for woodpeckers, but they are actually defying gravity. One of the special features making it possible for them to perform this incredible feat is the unique tail.

Tail feathers, called rectices, are the "third leg of the tripod" that makes a woodpecker stable while gripping a tree. A woodpecker's tail is composed of 12 feathers—6 pairs of feathers on opposite sides of center, with the center 2 feathers being the longest and strongest. These feathers have pointed tips, a reinforced shaft and extra strong barbs that interlock the smaller feather parts together. In addition, the ends of the feathers are curved inward slightly. This is a valuable asset that increases the surface pressure when the tail is propped against a tree.

Downy Woodpecker

Other birds molt their tail feathers from the center outward. To maintain maximum support, woodpeckers molt their tail feathers from the second innermost pair out. The longest, strongest and most important center pair is shed and replaced only after all outer feathers have been replaced and are in good working order.

Most woodpeckers have black tail feathers. The black color comes from melanin, a granular pigment that gives feathers extra strength and durability. White feathers lack the pigment and are weaker than black feathers. No woodpecker has all-white tail feathers.

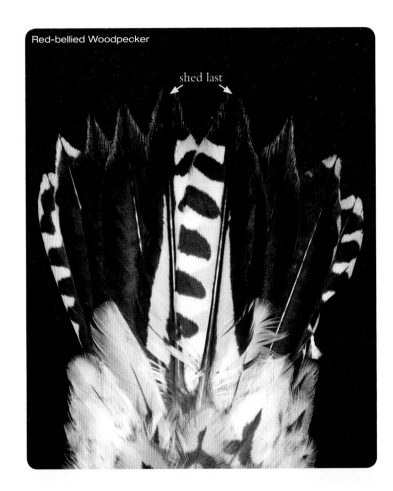

Red-bellied Woodpecker

shed last

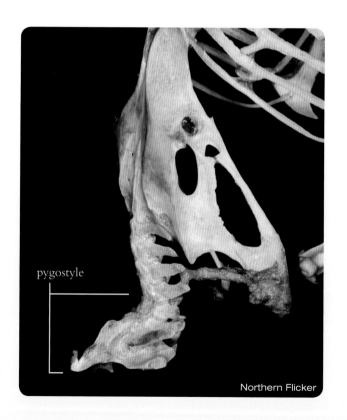

pygostyle

Northern Flicker

Considering the constant friction of a woodpecker's tail against the abrasive rough surfaces of a tree, strong tail feathers are essential. In addition to tail feather strength, a woodpecker needs strong muscles and bone structure to control and brace its tail against a tree.

Woodpeckers have modified tail muscles and enlarged bones to accommodate muscle attachment. The last six vertebrae in a bird's spinal column are fused together in a plow-shaped bone called the pygostyle. The size of this bone is directly proportional to how much a bird uses its tail, so in woodpeckers it is very large. Woodpeckers that spend a lot of time aerial foraging for food, such as Lewis's Woodpeckers and flickers, have a smaller pygostyle. Black-backed and American Three-toed Woodpeckers have the largest pygostyles since they spend all of their time clinging to the sides of trees.

Black-backed Woodpecker

Moving up and down a tree only seems easy because woodpeckers make it look that way. The force of gravity, however, is constantly working against these tree climbers. Once a woodpecker lands on a tree, it needs to move up or down to search for food. This is accomplished by "hitching up the tree trunk." The process starts when a woodpecker draws its body toward the tree and uses its legs to lunge upward. At this point the bird partially releases itself from the tree with its feet, but still keeps contact with its tail. The tail acts like a spring, helping to propel the bird upward. These combined actions are so fast and effortless that it's not possible to see them with the naked eye. A slow-motion video is needed to see everything involved in hitching.

Woodpeckers also have the ability to hitch down a tree. This is even more complicated because the woodpecker can't see where it is going when moving downward.

Black-backed Woodpecker

Sapsuckers tend to hold their bodies close to tree trunks while hitching, causing their tails to be nearly in continual contact with trees. Black-backed Woodpeckers normally hold their bodies farther away from trunks and use their tails as a spring much more than other woodpeckers.

American Three-toed Woodpecker

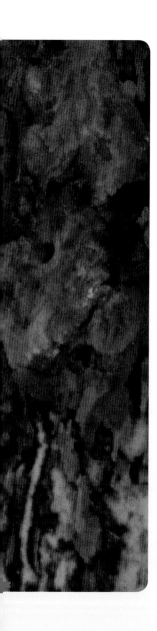

WHAT'S FOR DINNER?

Insects are the main food source for all species of woodpeckers. Eggs, larvae and adults of nearly every insect species are fair game, along with a wide variety of spiders. Ants and beetles are the forage food of choice of many woodpecker species.

In some species, such as flickers, ants make up the majority of the diet. Stomach content studies of nearly 700 flickers showed that 98 percent of the birds had ants and no other food in their stomachs. One stomach contained over 5,000 ants. Another had over 3,000.

Like flickers, Black-backed Woodpeckers and American Three-toed Woodpeckers are also food specialists, but they concentrate their gathering efforts on beetle larvae. A Black-backed Woodpecker will spend many hours at a tree, tearing off bark in search of wood-boring pine beetle larvae. This work results in a mound of freshly chiseled bark at the tree base. An American Three-toed Woodpecker will dig out bark beetle larvae, which is much the same activity and leaves similar evidence as the Black-backed.

Some woodpeckers occasionally dine on bird eggs and nestlings. Red-bellied Woodpeckers videotaped by this author, for example, entered a Wood Duck box, but didn't take over the cavity—they just pecked a hole in an egg and lapped up the yoke. These same birds also poked holes in a full clutch of Eastern Screech-Owl eggs. Red-bellies are also known to take small nestlings out of a nest and swallow them whole. Honestly, it's a bird-eat-bird world out there!

Red-bellied Woodpecker

HAWKING

Some woodpeckers hunt like predators for food instead of foraging. A Red-headed Woodpecker, for instance, will often perch perpendicularly on a tree branch and wait for a flying insect. After spotting one, the bird will quickly fly out, snatch it in midair and return to the branch to eat, where it remains until the next delicious bite passes by. This method of hunting is called hawking and is more commonly seen in flycatchers and other small birds.

Red-headed Woodpecker

THE FOOD PANTRY

Of the nearly 200 species of true woodpeckers, only a handful cache food for later consumption. There are two ways that woodpeckers store food. Scatter hoarders, such as Red-bellied Woodpeckers, take tiny bits of food and store them in a haphazard way in cracks of tree branches and trunks. Since these small caches are hidden randomly, there is no way to defend them from marauding squirrels or other birds. Larder hoarders stockpile large amounts of food in a single location. Since their entire stash of food is stored in one place, the pantry needs defending.

Red-bellied Woodpecker

Acorn Woodpecker granary

The Acorn Woodpecker is the woodpecker king of food storage. This bird spends an inordinate amount of time drilling acorn-sized holes in trees. The storage area as a whole is called a granary. Each Acorn Woodpecker family has a primary storage tree and up to six secondary locations. In late summer and fall, the family busily fills the empty storage holes with acorns. This will provide enough provisions for the winter. Also, collecting acorns into a central granary makes it easier to protect their food from squirrels and trespassing birds. A typical acorn granary consists of several thousand holes, perfectly sized and shaped. Given that it takes one woodpecker about one hour to drill a hole, a family of five could create about 500 holes in one year. It takes several years to create a very large granary, and Acorn Woodpeckers fiercely defend it from squirrels and birds. Other times, unfortunately, these woodpeckers will use wood trim on homes and other buildings for their larder instead of trees.

Acorn Woodpecker granary

Lewis's Woodpecker

Lewis's, Red-bellied and Red-headed Woodpeckers also stockpile food to eat later, but to a slightly lesser extent. Lewis's Woodpeckers gather pine nuts, acorns, corn kernels and other seeds and nuts and tuck them into natural cracks and crevices. They may get several dozen food items into a crevice, but they don't create huge stockpiles like Acorn Woodpeckers. Lewis's Woodpeckers also defend their crack larders from other birds since they store their food in one basic location in their territory.

Red-headed Woodpecker

Red-headed Woodpeckers cooperate in family units to cache food, storing food bits in cracks of trees. Red-heads stash large numbers of nuts in natural cavities or even in old nest cavities. They also have been known to stock insects for later consumption.

Yellow-bellied Sapsucker

74

Sapsuckers are a group of woodpeckers that drill a series of small holes in trees to release the sweet sap beneath the bark. These holes are called taps or wells. When sapsuckers migrate back to their territory in spring, they typically pick an aspen, birch or maple tree and drill a series of small round or oval holes in a straight line around the trunk, from which the sap leaks. Sapsuckers lap up the sap with their specialized tongues, which are tipped with hairs, like a paintbrush. Sap represents about 20–30 percent of a sapsucker's total diet. After capturing a beakful of insects, sapsuckers often dip the prey into the sap before feeding it to their young, presumably to establish the lifelong sap diet.

Yellow-bellied Sapsucker

Sapsuckers are not the only species attracted to flowing sap taps. Insects also congregate to get a sip, and sapsuckers and other birds take advantage of this, snapping up the bugs. Hummingbirds, warblers and other birds use the taps not only to gather insects, but to drink the sap as well.

Once a line or series of holes dries and scabs, sapsuckers will drill a fresh set of holes just above or below the area to start the sap flowing again. This leads to many lines or series of holes in one tree. After the birds stop using the taps, the holes close and heal without permanent damage to the tree.

Red-spotted Purple Butterfly

Ruby-throated Hummingbird

PREENING

Woodpeckers need to preen and clean their feathers like other birds, but since woodpecker feathers tend to be stiffer, they don't have to spend as much time at this job. A typical preening session lasts just a few minutes. As a woodpecker clings to a tree or perches, it grabs an untidy feather and pulls to straighten it or zip together the parts that had become separated during daily activity.

Nuttall's Woodpecker

Golden-fronted Woodpecker

QUICK BATHS

Woodpeckers are also not big-time bathers. Clean, well-tended feathers are important, and while woodpeckers don't ignore personal hygiene, they don't need to maintain their feathers like birds with softer feathers. Many birds, such as American Robins and Blue Jays, are often seen taking complete baths. Woodpeckers take only short baths, usually at shallow puddles, birdbaths and lake edges. Sometimes they'll sit out in a rainstorm and take a shower.

Yellow-bellied Sapsucker

SUNNING

Sunbathing is seen more often in other bird species, but woodpeckers do it, too. If you notice a woodpecker draped on a branch in a trance-like state, the bird is not sleeping—it's taking a sun bath. When sunning, the woodpecker droops its wings, raises its head, opens its beak and fluffs the feathers on its back and rump, exposing the skin beneath. After a minute or two, the bird will appear to awaken, gather itself up and fly off when fully alert. Sunbathing must feel good and is thought to help rid the skin of mites and ticks.

CALL NOTES

Most people are familiar with bird songs, but not calls—and there is an important distinction between the two. A song is a series of musical notes strung together into a cohesive melody. A call is usually a single-note unmusical sound that is repeated over and over. The vocal repertoire of woodpeckers is limited just to calls. No woodpecker produces a song, but all have a wide variety of calls. In all woodpeckers, the call note becomes more repetitious with the bird's excitement level and increases in intensity as the agitation of the bird grows. Calls often communicate locations to mates and other family members. Nearly all woodpecker species have a 1-note call, but some have more. The White-headed Woodpecker, for instance, has a 2-note or occasionally a 3-note call. Woodpeckers call anytime of year, but call notes are given more frequently during breeding season when squabbles over territories and mates are fairly common.

White-headed Woodpecker

Territorial calls of Pileated Woodpeckers, Northern Flickers and other large woodpeckers are very loud and given during spring to announce possession of a territory. These calls are distinctive and quite obvious. They are often repeated for many hours, usually in early morning and again in the evening. Some of these calls are so interesting, they are used as background sound in Hollywood movies.

Northern Flicker

DRUMMING TO COMMUNICATE

Most woodpeckers will drum as a means of communication. Drumming is the act of rapidly striking the tip of the bill against a branch, trunk, or hollow object that resonates, often for just a few seconds. Most drumming consists of a rapid series of taps (usually too fast for people to count) that increases with the bird's excitement or distress. Woodpeckers drum mainly during breeding season, and both sexes participate. Similar to birds that sing, woodpeckers drum to announce the possession of territory, to attract a mate and as a feature of courtship. Some species combine drumming with calling for additional emphasis. Sapsuckers drum in a slow, erratic pattern unlike other woodpeckers, making them easy to identify by their drumming alone.

Red-bellied Woodpecker

Yellow-bellied Sapsucker

Drumming is accomplished with the neck muscles, which are very strong. The body remains still and locked in position while the head and bill quickly raps the sound. The key to successful drumming is to select a branch, trunk, man-made hollow item or an object with little water content so the sound amplifies and resonates, carrying the message throughout the forest. Drumming doesn't produce holes in trees, and the same locations are used repeatedly. Some especially good spots are used for several years. During non-breeding season, drumming decreases dramatically.

Drumming on house chimneys or stovepipes is very common. It should come as no surprise why woodpeckers choose these items for drumming since amplification carries the sound very far indeed.

Studies of woodpecker drumming indicate that the tempo (beats per second) says much about the bird to other woodpeckers. Drumming relays information about the species, the bird's sex and emotional state such as level of stimulation or anxiety. While the exact meaning of woodpecker drumming is lost on people, the nuances apparently speak volumes to the birds.

Red-headed Woodpecker

Williamson's Sapsucker

SAPSUCKER MIGRATION

Woodpeckers are hardy birds, well equipped to survive winter. There is no reason for most species to migrate to warmer regions since they are experts at finding insect eggs, larvae and seeds, even during cold weather. Sapsuckers, however, which are much more dependent on insects and also need tree sap, must migrate south. When the weather starts turning cold in the fall, sapsuckers begin to move south. They spend their winters in the lowest tier of states, Mexico and some Caribbean islands, including Cuba and Jamaica, where there is relatively warm weather and a constant supply of insects. Sapsuckers start heading north in spring, timing their arrival with the initial flow of sap and emergence of the first insects.

WOODPECKER TERRITORIES

Most woodpecker species are not migratory, meaning they occupy their territory all year long. However, that doesn't mean they defend territory year-round. Establishing and defending a territory occurs only in late winter and spring.

All woodpeckers audibly claim a territory with a combination of loud repetitive calls and drumming on hollow branches, logs and trunks. Most territory announcements are performed by the male. When territorial rivals come into close proximity, vocal displays switch to visual displays. Visual displays involve feather fluffing, wing spreading and tail flaring, all to appear larger and more powerful. When the visuals don't work, there is physical contact between rivals, but this is usually superficial and lasts only a few seconds.

Red-cockaded Woodpecker

The smaller the woodpecker, the smaller the territory. The small Downy Woodpecker, for example, controls only ½–1 acre. The Ladder-backed Woodpecker, a bigger bird contending with limited food in desert habitat, defends a larger territory to ensure a constant food supply. The Pileated Woodpecker, our largest woodpecker, commands a very large territory of up to several square miles. A Pileated spends much of the day moving through its territory in search of food, visiting suet and seed feeders only every couple days after making the rounds.

Woodpeckers defend their territories against others of their own species, not against all other woodpeckers. Thus, a Pileated won't spend much time chasing off a Downy or Hairy Woodpecker that has made its home within the Pileated's larger territory.

Ladder-backed Woodpecker

Northern Flicker

NEST—NEW OR OLD?

Woodpeckers are masters at excavating holes in trees. Cavity nesting affords woodpeckers and their families protective advantages against inclement weather and many kinds of predators. As a result, woodpecker eggs and hatchlings have a higher rate of survival compared with open-nesting birds such as warblers.

All woodpeckers utilize cavities in trees for nesting, but not all woodpeckers excavate their own holes. Cavities can be natural or made by other woodpeckers. Using an existing cavity not only saves precious energy, it enables a bird to devote more time to mating and raising young. The Northern Flicker is a good example of a woodpecker that usually will choose an existing nest cavity for its home. Flickers often compete with bluebirds, flycatchers and other birds for the limited supply of vacant homes. Unlike songbirds, however, when an existing hole is not available, flickers will excavate their own. In addition, they will often return to the same cavity year after year.

Red-naped Sapsucker

While it makes sense that nesting in an old cavity saves effort and energy, studies showed that sapsucker pairs using old nest cavities fledged fewer babies than sapsuckers nesting in freshly excavated holes. These findings conflicted with the fact that the sapsuckers using old cavities produced more eggs. Most likely the lower fledging success is because of the parasite load left over from previous years.

Red-headed Woodpecker

SPECIALIZED CAVITIES

Some woodpeckers, such as the Red-headed Woodpecker, excavate several cavities around their territory and use them all year. They'll make one for nesting, some for roosting and others for storing food, hiding in any as needed for emergency protection against avian predators such as Cooper's Hawks.

Like the Red-heads, Red-cockaded Woodpeckers also use their nest cavities year-round. However, Red-cockadeds return to the cavity each evening, where the entire family sleeps together—a very unusual behavior since most woodpeckers excavate a cavity only to incubate eggs and raise young. Unlike Red-cockadeds, once other young woodpeckers leave the nest (fledge), they typically don't come back to the cavity again.

Red-cockaded Woodpecker

Northern Flicker

Pileated Woodpecker

CHOOSING A NEST SITE

No one knows why a woodpecker chooses a particular tree for nest excavation. We can only speculate as to how a woodpecker judges a tree for its interior heartwood. Maybe it looks for fungal fruiting bodies (mushrooms) on the bark, which indicate soft heartwood. Perhaps snapped limbs or broken branches are a signal that the tree is a suitable place for construction. The woodpecker may also tap on a trunk, listening and judging for density or hollowness.

In all woodpecker species, there may be several false starts to nest cavity construction. A pair will start excavating, but might discontinue the work a quarter to halfway into the project and fly off to try another location. The White-headed Woodpecker is well known for this behavior. It could be that White-heads need extremely specific sites that are hard to find, and that the only way to choose the best one is to start excavating and move on if the location proves deficient.

White-headed Woodpecker

woodpecker holes

Some individuals complete a cavity and then will not use it. The reasons for this occurrence range from lack of experience to a perceived danger to the loss of a mate or partner.

Some woodpecker species prefer a specific tree limb or trunk and return to it for many years. Each year they excavate a new hole a few feet below or above the previous year's cavity. This is often the case with Red-bellied, Red-headed, Pileated and Gila Woodpeckers.

Downy Woodpecker

CAVITY EXCAVATION

The male woodpecker usually starts the nest excavation. First, he will choose a territory with several potential nest trees. Next, he calls loudly from high perches and drums on hollow branches within his territory to advertise his availability and desire to mate.

Normally, the male also selects the nest site. Most woodpeckers search for dead branches and trunks to excavate, presumably because dead wood is softer. Other woodpeckers, such as Pileated and Red-cockaded Woodpeckers, frequently opt for live trees. Red-headed Woodpeckers and other species excavate their nest cavities just below a large branch or prominent shelf fungus, which give their cavity openings additional protection from rain.

The initial hole is a simple cone-shaped depression only an inch or so deep. When the male successfully attracts a mate, he will bring her to the proposed dwelling site. If she accepts it, the male continues to carve out the cavity. The division of labor falls mainly on the male, but the female will help. Cavity preparation is apparently essential for building a strong pair bond. If the male falls behind in his work or if the female is getting close to laying eggs, the female will pitch in to help speed construction.

During nest chamber construction, excavated wood chips go flying in all directions. Most species make no attempt to hide the chips or carry away the excess. Wood chips simply fall to the ground as they are chiseled out during the initial excavation. When the cavity becomes large enough for the adult to be halfway inside, the bird will back out, along with assorted chips that fall out of the hole. Later, when working fully in the interior, the adult will gather a beakful of chips, poke its head out of the cavity and spit out the chips to be carried away on the wind.

Downy Woodpecker

Red-headed Woodpecker

Downy Woodpecker

Pileated Woodpecker cavity

CHAMBER ENTRANCE

The trick to the circumference of the cavity entrance hole is to keep it as small as possible and still allow the parents to come and go, while keeping out predators. The Downy Woodpecker makes the smallest entrance hole, chiseling it perfectly round. A Pileated Woodpecker nest entrance is the largest, approximately 4 inches, with a roughly triangular or oval shape.

Nest entrance size is important because it buffers the interior from bad weather and keeps out predators such as raccoons. If you spend time watching a woodpecker nest cavity, you'll see that the adults just barely fit through the opening. In fact, they often have to squeeze in and out with an extra wiggle or push. While a small entrance helps to keep the nest safe, the unfortunate consequence of entering and leaving the cavity through such a limited space is weakened feathers with a shorter life span.

ROOSTING HABITS

In the same way that a cavity gives woodpeckers an advantage reproductively, it also provides the birds with a safe, warm and reliable place to sleep. Nearly all woodpecker species roost in cavities at night and almost never use them for sleeping purposes during the day. Daytime cavity use is strictly reserved for egg laying and raising young.

Most woodpecker species have 3–4 cavities designated just for nocturnal roosting. Studies of Pileated Woodpeckers in the Pacific Northwest showed that they use up to a dozen different nighttime roosts. This practice ensures that if a cavity is temporarily filled by a trespasser or the tree blows down in a storm, the homeowner can choose one of several backup places in which to spend the night. Depending on territory size, extra roosting cavities may be scattered over many acres.

Yellow-bellied Sapsucker

Acorn Woodpecker

Even when a primary cavity is not damaged or taken over by another bird, most woodpecker species will roost in a different cavity every 3–4 days. Moving intermittently to different cavities reduces the chances of a predator taking advantage of a known roost. Many woodpeckers will abandon their nocturnal roost if a predator disturbs them, with some leaving at the sound of a mammal climbing the tree trunk.

Unlike Red-cockaded Woodpeckers and Acorn Wood-peckers, most woodpecker species roost alone. Every night year-round, family units of Red-cockadeds roost together in their main cavity. In the woodpecker world, this is extremely peculiar behavior indeed! Acorn Woodpeckers also roost with each other on any night and in any season. The average number of roosting Acorns is three, but groups of more than a dozen have been recorded.

More than one body inside a cavity goes a long way to help keep the air warm. In one study where the outside air temperature was 32 °F and the inside temperature of an unoccupied nest cavity showed 40 °F, the inside temperature of another cavity with four woodpeckers sharing it reached 50 °F. Collective body heat was thus proven to be very effective at raising the internal temperature of a cavity. Sapsuckers are the least likely woodpeckers to use a cavity for sleep. Female sapsuckers almost always sleep openly on a tree trunk, occasionally sheltered by over-hanging leaves. Male sapsuckers, such as the Yellow-bellied Sapsucker, roost in a cavity only during mating season. This is especially true from the time eggs are laid to when the young leave the nest (fledge).

Roosting woodpeckers don't settle down on the cavity floor to sleep. Instead, they cling to an interior wall and tuck their beaks under a wing in much the same way as a duck or other bird sleeps. Woodpeckers that don't use roosting cavities simply cling to the vertical surfaces of trees and tuck their bills under a wing.

Pileated Woodpecker

Golden-fronted Woodpecker

VISUAL DISPLAYS

Visual displays, which include courtship displays, are common in woodpeckers. All woodpecker species employ a wide variety of visual displays to convey messages of attraction, aggression and defense. Displays of affection and antagonism are very similar and nearly impossible to tell apart. Almost all are accompanied by a vocalization and are intrasexual, meaning males display and vocalize to other males, and females do the same to other females.

A common woodpecker display is wing spreading and crest raising. Spread wings increases the appearance of body size and often exposes brightly colored feathers. Raising the crest feathers on top of the head accentuates sexual identity. The males of most woodpecker species show a sexual difference by a mark on the head, back or throat, and an upright crest helps to display the male gender. Once the wings are spread and head feathers are raised, the male will sometimes turn his head back and forth to further flaunt the markings.

Bill pointing is a display performed by both woodpecker males and females. During this competition, opposing woodpeckers hold a pose with their heads extended and bills pointed directly at each other. The "winner"—the dominant bird—will eventually hold its bill higher than the submissive opponent.

Bobbing and bowing is another classic woodpecker display. It involves raising and lowering the head, alternated with swinging the body from side to side. Often the woodpecker will trace circles or figure eights in the air with the point of its bill afterward. Wing and tail spreading are also common in this display.

Downy Woodpecker

Red-bellied Woodpecker

MATING ENCOUNTERS

Mating encounters between male and female woodpeckers are really not much different from any other bird. For a period of up to two weeks before egg laying begins, the pair may copulate many times during the day, typically in quick succession. These encounters are thought to help strengthen the pair bond rather than fertilize eggs. This mating usually occurs after an encounter with a male or female woodpecker that has intruded into the couple's territory.

Mating generally takes place on or near the nest tree, with the actual coupling almost always occurring on a horizontal branch or broken trunk. Either sex initiates the encounter. It often starts with drumming or loud calling from the designated copulation perch. Normally, the male flies to the female, who is positioned perpendicular to the perch. She will crouch down and lift her tail while the male stands on her back, fluttering. While her tail is lifted, the male curls his tail down until the two reproductive organs (cloaca) touch in what is known as a cloacal kiss, and culminates in a sperm packet passing to the female. All of this takes only seconds. Afterward, the male flitters off, landing on a nearby perch. Preening and general feather care usually follow these sessions.

Red-bellied Woodpecker

Downy Woodpecker eggs

WHITE EGGSHELLS

The color of bird eggs is an intriguing topic. Many ground-nesting birds, such as Killdeer, produce decorated eggs that blend into the surroundings. Killdeer camouflage is so good, the eggs are nearly impossible to see. In the woodpecker world, all species produce white or nearly white eggs. It is assumed that camouflage is unnecessary because eggs in a cavity are not visible to predators—not to mention that the cavity is constantly dark. Some believe the white color helps the parents see the eggs within the dim light of the cavity, which would reduce the chances of accidental egg breakage.

SMALL EGGS

Compared with adult body size and mass, woodpeckers have relatively small eggs. Downy Woodpecker eggs, for instance, are only ½ inch long and weigh less than ¹⁄₁₀ ounce. By comparison, the eggs of Northern Flickers are ¾ inch long. Pileated Woodpecker eggs are the largest, with a length of 1 inch.

EGGS ON SCHEDULE

The egg laying schedule is the same in woodpeckers as it is in other birds. Female woodpeckers lay one egg each day, and occasionally one every other day. Egg laying usually takes place early in the morning, but woodpeckers can lay eggs at any hour in the nest cavity because they are constantly and safely concealed.

Red-headed Woodpecker

Birds that lay only a specific number of eggs are known as determinate egg layers. No matter what misfortune happens to the eggs during the laying period, even if all eggs get destroyed, determinate egg-laying birds cannot replace any of the lost eggs with new ones.

Woodpeckers are indeterminate egg layers, meaning that the number of eggs a female woodpecker can lay is not limited. If some eggs get damaged or disappear during the egg laying period, the female will keep laying replacement eggs until she reaches a full-sized clutch. One female Red-headed Woodpecker, for example, laid a total of more than 30 eggs in one breeding season after losing all of her original eggs to an illegal egg collector. (Collecting bird eggs of any type has been illegal for many years.)

Hairy Woodpecker

CLUTCH DIVERSITY

In a normal nesting season, Hairy Woodpeckers usually lay
up to 6 eggs. The egg maximum for Pileated Woodpeckers
is slightly higher, at 7–8 per nest. The upper limit for Lewis's
Woodpeckers is 9 eggs, while Red-headed Woodpeckers
normally top out at 10 eggs per clutch.

Arizona Woodpecker

Many factors contribute to the diversity of average clutch size. Female age is key, with older females producing larger clutches, presumably because older birds have more reserves for egg production in their bodies than the younger females. Habitat quality and resulting food resources also impact egg numbers. A female with abundant food will produce more eggs on average than another bird with limited food.

Weather is another issue that affects egg production. Females lay more eggs during years with warm weather and lots of insects than in cold, wet years with fewer bugs. Latitude also plays a role. Woodpeckers in northern latitudes average more eggs per clutch than their southern counterparts. Woodpeckers living in the tropics tend toward the smallest egg numbers, with many species producing only 2–3 eggs per clutch. This phenomenon is still not well understood.

Northern Flicker

INCUBATION DAY AND NIGHT

Woodpeckers are dedicated and diligent parents even before their baby birds hatch, starting with the first stage of incubation, called mock incubation. The female can lay at most only one egg each day, so it takes many days to lay a full clutch. While the eggs are being laid, the female and male will alternately sit on the eggs for short periods, with each rotation usually lasting under 30 minutes. At all times, one parent is either incubating eggs or standing by the nest cavity, guarding the eggs. The mock incubation period usually lasts 7–10 days, depending on the number of eggs laid.

Genuine incubation starts only after all eggs are laid. It's easy to tell when this begins because one parent will continually sit on the eggs. Parents switch incubation duty, usually every couple hours, which allows the sitting bird to leave the cavity, stretch, defecate and find some food. Relief time can last from five minutes to several hours. The switch itself is a fast, hushed activity initiated by the returning mate, who will softly tap the tree as a heads-up or give quiet, intimate calls.

In nearly all bird species, the female is the primary incubator overnight. In woodpeckers, however, the male is the primary nocturnal incubator. This is very unusual behavior in the bird world, and another unique aspect of this fascinating group of birds.

Acorn Woodpecker

BROOD PATCH

In all woodpecker species, a brood patch develops in both the female and the male. A brood patch is a small region on the upper belly and lower breast of a bird. It has a rich supply of blood vessels that run just beneath the surface of the skin. The small downy feathers underneath the larger feathers fall out, exposing bare skin. The naked skin touches the eggs, allowing for effective heat transfer from the parents to the eggs and also to the baby birds later, during brooding. In most bird species, the male lacks a brood patch and can only temporarily help the female keep eggs warm. In woodpeckers, the male develops a vascularized skin patch just like the female, giving him the ability to share equally in warming duties.

In select woodpecker species, such as the Acorn Woodpecker and Red-cockaded Woodpecker, some family members help the parents incubate or brood and will consequently develop a brood patch. These brood patches are much less developed than those of the breeding pair.

TEMPERATURE CONTROL

Cavity-nesting birds enjoy relatively stable and moderate temperatures within the nesting cavity. Compared with outside temperatures, nest cavities are warmer in cold weather and cooler in hot weather. However, if it gets too cold within the cavity, parents keep the eggs warm by expending extra energy. Compensating actions include fluffing the feathers, sitting tightly on the eggs and taking fewer breaks. When it becomes too warm in the cavity, parents metabolize more water than usual, which increases humidity and allows for some cooling.

Gilded Flicker

TIME TO HATCH

Woodpeckers have many unique features, and egg hatching is no exception. All members of the woodpecker family have a shorter incubation period than other birds of comparable size, ranging from 4–6 fewer days. Most North American woodpecker species incubate for a total of 10–15 days. This does not include the mock incubation period of 7–10 days.

The reason for shorter incubation in woodpeckers is related to the amount of oxygen in the nest cavity. When the young are encased in the egg, there is a constant exchange of oxygen and carbon dioxide through the eggshell. The gas exchange effectiveness diminishes gradually as the parents incubate, because their respiratory action lowers the oxygen level in the cavity and increases the carbon dioxide. In addition, incoming fresh air is hindered by the cavity nest itself, which has only one entrance hole. By the time the gas exchange through the eggshell is sufficiently reduced, the young are ready to hatch. Gas exchange efficiency is no longer an issue once the babies are hatched and breathing on their own inside the cavity.

A shorter incubation period means that baby woodpeckers hatch in a more immature state than other baby birds. Because they are more immature, it also means that their parents will need to stay with them in the nest cavity for an equally longer period. All eggs in a nest hatch within a day or two of each other. When the hatchlings emerge, they are naked and helpless, with eyes and ears sealed shut. The only thing they can do is lift their heads and open their mouths to be fed. Within 24 hours, however, baby woodpeckers are using the cavity walls to crawl up to the entrance to beg for food.

Downy Woodpecker — newly hatched

COOPERATIVE BROODING

Feeding the young and continuing to keep them warm is a full-time job for the parents during the first week of hatchling life. Newly hatched woodpecker babies have translucent pink skin and no feathers. At this stage they are so immature, their ability to regulate their own body temperature is nonfunctional, and the parents must keep them warm. Both the male and female will alternately sit on the hatchlings in a warming process called brooding. Brooding (from which comes the phrase "brooding mother") lasts 5–7 days or until the developing thermoregulation system is working, and the youngsters have enough feathers to retain the warmth they create.

During the brooding period, the parent delivering food to the babies will first feed them, then quickly sit on them. When the other parent appears at the cavity with food and is ready to provide brooding relief, the sitting parent leaves to stretch, defecate and collect more insects. This tag team approach goes on all day long.

Downy Woodpecker — day 6

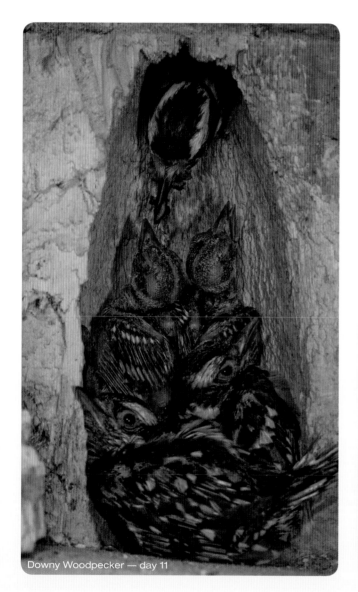

Downy Woodpecker — day 11

Downy Woodpecker — day 13

FEEDING THE YOUNG

All members of the woodpecker family feed their young a diet of insects. Insects are a protein-packed food that fuels fast growth in young woodpeckers. The adult birds stop brooding at the end of the first week, but continue to deliver food. At this time the parents spend the majority of their time looking for food, searching every crack and crevice for soft-bodied insects, such as caterpillars, spiders and flies, to bring back to their family.

Parents returning with food will land at the cavity entrance with brimming beakfuls of assorted insects. Adults often will pause and look around for danger before entering the cavity. The young are large enough by this time to take up most of the cavity space. Thus, adults enter the cavity only halfway, leaving their tails hanging out. They will quickly tip in and out of the cavity, each time delivering some of the insect payload to a baby. Parents don't try to distribute food equally. Instead, the baby bird that begs the most will get the most food.

Red-bellied Woodpecker

Gilded Flicker

Most woodpecker species deliver food to their young by the beakful. Others, such as the Gilded Flicker, Northern Flicker and Pileated Woodpecker, cache food in a specialized expandable pouch in the esophagus, called the crop.

Parents regurgitate food from the crop directly into the mouths of their begging babies. The adult inserts its long bill into the open and waiting mouth of a baby, interlocking beaks before delivering the food. Not all of the crop content is delivered at once. Instead, a parent will dole it out piecemeal among the waiting mouths.

Woodpeckers transport more food in their crops than other woodpeckers can in their beaks. As a result, regurgitating birds make fewer trips to and from the nest. Most of these birds visit the cavity only about once every hour. Woodpeckers carrying food in their bills make many more trips in an hour. Some studies have shown that parents bringing food in their beaks visit the cavity 5–10 times per hour. However, one particularly energetic pair of Red-bellied Woodpeckers was reported to deliver beakfuls of food at a much higher rate—an astonishing 40 times per hour!

Red-bellied Woodpecker

Feeding is usually the most intense during the first few hours after sunrise and again several hours before sunset. When young woodpeckers are fairly large and demanding even more food, the parents will be much more active, ferrying food to the nest cavity nonstop throughout the day. However, if morning temperatures are cool or cold, insects are inactive and feeding will be delayed until the air warms.

Gila Woodpecker

Northern Flicker

FECAL SACS

After a beakful of insects is delivered, sometimes the adult will enter the cavity fully and emerge a few seconds later with other objects in its bill that look like bugs. These are actually fecal sacs, not insects. After the young feed, the babies will turn around and raise their tails, exposing the vent (cloaca). The parent bringing food will grab fecal sacs as the young excrete them in an effort to keep the cavity interior clean. After gathering several sacs, one from each baby, the parent will fly off and drop them away from the nest. In some species, adults take fecal sacs to a tree away from the cavity, where they will wipe them off on a branch.

Pileated Woodpecker

By the time a young woodpecker leaves the nest, or fledges, it is the same size as the adults. In most species, it also sports the same plumage. In addition to appearing like the adults, most young woodpeckers sound like the adults as well. Young Pileated Woodpeckers, for instance, look and sound just like adults when they leave the nest. The Red-headed Woodpecker, on the other hand, is a good example of a species in which the young appear different from the adults, with brown heads instead of red.

juvenile Red-headed Woodpecker

Red-headed Woodpecker

INDEPENDENCE

For 7–10 days after leaving the nest cavity, young woodpeckers follow the adults around and beg for food. When one of the parents approaches, the fledglings will squat and flutter their wings, holding open their mouths to be fed. This is standard posture for food begging. Parents will deliver a beakful of insects and then fly off to find more. Near the end of the fledgling period, the young birds start to find insects by themselves and begging decreases. Soon the young woodpeckers are completely independent and searching for their own food.

Red-headed Woodpecker

136

Downy Woodpecker

ATTRACTING WOODPECKERS

Attracting woodpeckers to your yard is as simple as putting up a bird feeder. The first thing you will need to consider is the location. Position the feeding station where you will be able to see and enjoy the visitors from a comfortable spot in your home.

To attract more than one species at a time, consider the kind of food to offer and the number of feeders. Woodpeckers like shelled peanuts or suet. Shelled peanuts are simply peanuts removed from their shells. Peanut feeders come in all sorts of shapes, colors and sizes, and any filled with fresh peanuts will easily draw woodpeckers. A sturdy wire feeder is best, with holes just large enough for the birds to extract one peanut at a time.

Downy Woodpecker

Setting out suet is another great way to bring in woodpeckers from the area. Suet is rendered beef fat and often contains other ingredients such as peanuts or birdseed. Some suet contains dried fruit or even insect parts. The fat content of suet is a fast, rich energy source that woodpeckers relish. Inexpensive metal wire cages are specially made to hold cakes or blocks of suet. Woodpeckers will cling to the cages, peck at the suet and knock off a chunk. They will either eat the morsel immediately or carry it off to enjoy at a nearby tree.

You can make your own suet, but since homemade cakes will get rancid in hot weather, it's best to offer those only during colder months. Many types of specialized, manufactured suet cakes or blocks won't spoil during warm weather and can be set out year-round.

Peanuts can be offered in every season. Providing peanuts or suet in an easily accessible feeder will ensure that many wonderful woodpeckers will be visiting your yard all year long.

Golden-fronted Woodpecker

Woodpeckers are a remarkable group of birds. From their ability to carve holes in solid trees, to their gravity-defying capacity to cling to trees, to every unique feat in between, woodpeckers deserve our attention and admiration. Easily drawn to our yards with a simple offering of suet or peanuts, we can appreciate these handsome birds year-round from the comfort of our homes. Woodpeckers are unlike all other bird species around the world, including the local birds that visit our feeding stations. For this reason and more, I continue to enjoy our incredible woodpeckers wherever they are found with amazement and delight.

Downy Woodpecker

FEATURED WOODPECKERS

This photo spread shows all 22 species of woodpeckers in the United States and Canada and their ranges. Ranges shown in brown indicate where you would most likely see resident woodpeckers during the year. Ranges for migration are shown in tan. Like other birds, woodpeckers move around freely and can be seen at different times of the year both inside and outside their ranges. Maps do not indicate the number of woodpeckers in a given area (density).

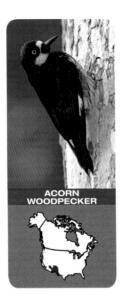

ACORN WOODPECKER

AMERICAN THREE-TOED WOODPECKER

ARIZONA WOODPECKER

BLACK-BACKED WOODPECKER

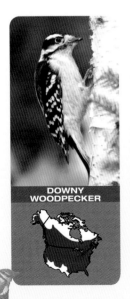

DOWNY WOODPECKER

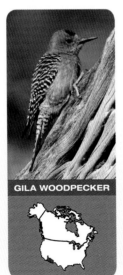

GILA WOODPECKER

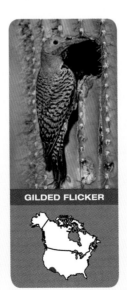

GILDED FLICKER

GOLDEN-FRONTED WOODPECKER

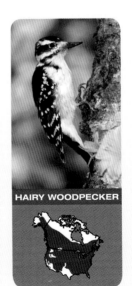

HAIRY WOODPECKER

LADDER-BACKED WOODPECKER

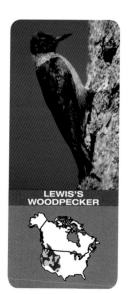

LEWIS'S WOODPECKER

NORTHERN FLICKER

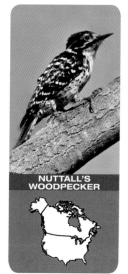

NUTTALL'S WOODPECKER

PILEATED WOODPECKER

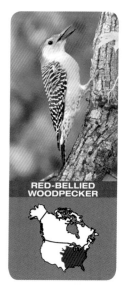

RED-BELLIED WOODPECKER

RED-BREASTED SAPSUCKER

RED-COCKADED WOODPECKER

RED-HEADED WOODPECKER

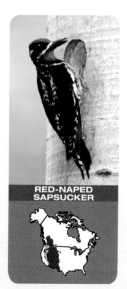

RED-NAPED SAPSUCKER

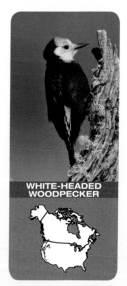

WHITE-HEADED WOODPECKER

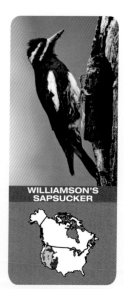

WILLIAMSON'S SAPSUCKER

YELLOW-BELLIED SAPSUCKER

ABOUT THE AUTHOR

Naturalist, wildlife photographer and writer Stan Tekiela is the originator of other popular nature appreciation books such as *Fascinating Loons: Amazing Images & Behaviors, Majestic Eagles: Compelling Facts and Images of the Bald Eagle, Captivating Bluebirds: Exceptional Images and Observations, Intriguing Owls: Exceptional Images and Insight* and *Amazing Hummingbirds: Unique Images and Characteristics*. For over two decades, Stan has authored more than 100 field guides and wildlife audio CDs for nearly every state in the nation, presenting many species of birds, mammals, reptiles and amphibians, trees, wildflowers and cacti. Holding a Bachelor of Science degree in Natural History from the University of Minnesota and as an active professional naturalist for more than 20 years, Stan studies and photographs wildlife throughout the United States and has received various national and regional awards for his books and photographs. Also a well-known columnist and radio personality, his syndicated column appears in more than 20 newspapers and his wildlife programs are broadcast on a number of Midwest radio stations. He is a member of the North American Nature Photography Association and Canon Professional Services. Stan lives in Victoria, Minnesota, with his wife, Katherine, and daughter, Abigail. He can be contacted via his web page at www.naturesmart.com.